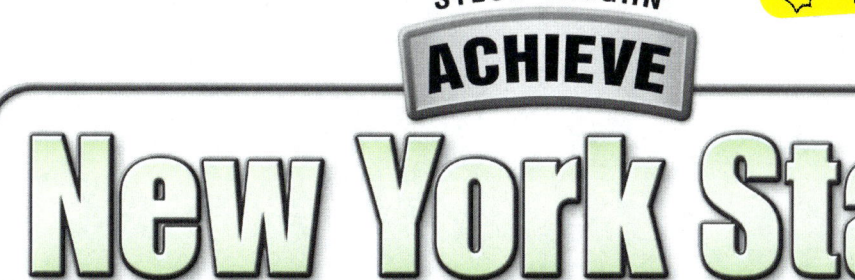

STECK-VAUGHN
ACHIEVE
New York State
Mathematics
5

Rigby • Saxon • Steck-Vaughn

www.HarcourtAchieve.com
1.800.531.5015

The New York State Testing Program Mathematics is published by CTB/McGraw-Hill. Such company has neither endorsed nor authorized this test-preparation book.

ISBN 978-1-4190-0949-5

© 2006 Harcourt Achieve Inc.

All rights reserved. No part of the material protected by this copyright may be reproduced or utilized in any form or by any means, in whole or in part, without permission in writing from the copyright owner. Requests for permission should be mailed to: Copyright Permissions, Harcourt Achieve, P.O. Box 27010, Austin, TX 78755.

Rigby and Steck-Vaughn are trademarks of Harcourt Achieve Inc. registered in the United States of America and/or other jurisdictions.

5 6 7 8 9 10 1413 15 14 13 12 11

4500310971

Achieve New York State Contents

New York State Mathematics Standards.................. 2
To the Student: About Achieve New York State........... 3

NYS Modeled Instruction 4
    Lesson 1   Number Sense and Operations 4
    Lesson 2   Algebra 18
    Lesson 3   Geometry 21
    Lesson 4   Measurement 28
    Lesson 5   Statistics and Probability................. 33

Practice Test for New York State Mathematics 35
    Session 1 35
    Session 2 49
    Cut-Out Tools..................................... 59
    NYS Testing Program Answer Sheet 61

New York State Mathematics Standards

Number Sense and Operations
- Understand numbers, different ways of writing numbers, how to work with numbers, and kinds of numbers.
- Understand types of operations and ways to solve problems.
- Solve problems correctly and make good estimates.

Algebra
- Represent and solve algebraically a wide range of problems.
- Solve algebra problems correctly.
- Recognize and use algebra patterns.

Geometry
- Identify shapes and solid figures.
- Identify and justify geometric relationships.
- Use knowledge of symmetry, flips, slides, and turns to solve problems.

Measurement
- Show what kinds of things can be measured and how to measure them.
- Use units of measurement.
- Estimate measurements.

Statistics and Probability
- Make and use sets of data.
- Make predictions that are based on data.

Process Strands
The Process Strands (Problem Solving, Reasoning and Proof, Communication, Connections, and Representation) describe ways of learning and using math knowledge. These Process Strands help to give meaning to math ideas and help link different math skills together. The Process Strands help to keep students interested in math. Students will understand and remember math better if they practice solving problems, know how different math ideas may have something in common, talk about math, make math connections, and model math ideas in different ways.

To the Student: About Achieve New York State

This book will help you prepare for the New York State Mathematics Test. The first part of the book lets you practice different kinds of questions you will see on the actual test. It also gives you a tip for answering each question.

The second part of the book is a practice test that is similar to the actual New York State Mathematics Test. Taking this practice test will help you know what the actual test is like.

The New York State Mathematics Test includes questions about Number Sense and Operations, Algebra, Geometry, Measurement, and Statistics and Probability. It will ask you to answer multiple-choice questions and use your ruler to measure objects. Test questions will help show how well you understand the math skills listed in the New York State Learning Standards.

Kinds of Questions

Multiple-Choice Questions

After each multiple-choice question are four answer choices. For the Modeled Instruction part of this book, you will circle the letter next to the correct answer. For the Practice Test, use the separate answer sheet, and fill in the circle that has the same letter as your answer.

Short- and Extended-Response Questions

These questions will not give you a choice to circle. You will need to read the problem and write out your own answer. There can be more than one correct answer to the problem. Sometimes you will need to draw a diagram or make a chart. You will also be asked to explain your answer in words or to show your work. It is important to show all your work as well as your final answer. You may receive partial credit if you have shown your work.

Lesson 1

Modeled Instruction
Number Sense and Operations

1 Mr. Carson lives in Auburn and works in Rochester. He drives 125 miles round-trip to work each day. Last year he worked 262 days. How many total miles did Mr. Carson drive to and from work last year?

- **A** 2,096
- **B** 26,200
- **C** 32,750
- **D** 65,500

Tip: *Round-trip* means the total distance to and from work. To find the total distance Mr. Carson drove to and from work last year, multiply the number of days he drove to and from work by the number of miles he drove per day.

2 What is the ratio of gray squares to white squares?

- **F** 5:7
- **G** 5:12
- **H** 7:5
- **J** 7:12

Tip: Ratios compare two amounts. To compare gray squares to white squares, first count the number of squares that are gray and then the number of squares that are white. Write the comparison in the correct order.

Go On

New York State Standards
1. Number Sense and Operations (Content 5.N.16, Process 5.PS.5)
   Use a variety of strategies to multiply three-digit numbers by three-digit numbers
2. Number Sense and Operations (Content 5.N.6, Process 5.PS.6)
   Understand the concept of ratio

4 ■ NYS Testing Program Modeled Instruction

3 Alison put 0.8 gallon of gasoline in her lawn mower. Which is another way to write this amount?

A $\frac{1}{5}$ gallon

B $\frac{2}{5}$ gallon

C $\frac{4}{5}$ gallon

D $\frac{8}{5}$ gallons

> **Tip:** Use place values to rewrite a decimal number as a fraction. The first place to the right of a decimal point is the tenths place. So, 0.8 is read as "eight tenths." Remember to write a fraction in simplest form.

4 $2\frac{1}{4} - 1\frac{3}{4}$

F $\frac{1}{2}$

G $\frac{7}{8}$

H 1

J $1\frac{5}{8}$

> **Tip:** Rewrite the mixed numbers as improper fractions with the same denominator. Then, use subtraction to solve the problem. Remember to write a fraction in simplest form.

New York State Standards
3. **Number Sense and Operations (Content 4.N.24, Process 5.R.6)** Express decimals as an equivalent form of fractions to tenths and hundredths (Post-March)
4. **Number Sense and Operations (Content 5.N.22, Process 5.CM.11)** Add and subtract mixed numbers with like denominators

Go On

5 Vladimir is keeping track of how much water he drinks. Yesterday he drank $\frac{5}{4}$ cups at school and $\frac{3}{4}$ cup after school. How many total cups of water did Vladimir drink yesterday?

A $\frac{2}{4}$ cup

B 1 cup

C $\frac{5}{4}$ cups

D 2 cups

> 🌀 **Tip:** Use addition to find the total amount. To add like fractions, add the numerators and keep the denominators the same. Simplify the result.

6 Nicole scored $\frac{92}{100}$ on her math test. What is Nicole's score written in lowest terms?

F $\frac{92}{25}$

G $\frac{9}{10}$

H $\frac{23}{25}$

J $\frac{23}{100}$

> 🌀 **Tip:** To write a fraction in lowest terms, find the greatest common factor. First list the factors of the numerator and the denominator, and find the greatest number that is in both lists. Then divide both the numerator and the denominator by the greatest common factor.

7 Four runners competed in a 100-yard dash. Their times are shown in the table below.

Runner	Time
Alia Miller	$12\frac{1}{2}$ seconds
Betty Gomez	$13\frac{1}{4}$ seconds
Charisse Halford	$12\frac{3}{8}$ seconds
Deanna Lee	$12\frac{5}{8}$ seconds

Which runner finished first?

A Alia Miller

B Betty Gomez

C Charisse Halford

D Deanna Lee

> 🌀 **Tip:** To compare fractions that have different denominators, rewrite them as equivalent fractions with a common denominator. Then compare the numerators.

New York State Standards
5. **Number Sense and Operations (Content 5.N.21, Process 5.PS.3)**
Use a variety of strategies to add and subtract fractions with like denominators
6. **Number Sense and Operations (Content 5.N.19, Process 5.R.6)**
Simplify fractions to lowest terms
7. **Number Sense and Operations (Content 5.N.5, Process 5.CN.8)**
Compare and order fractions including unlike denominators (with and without the use of a number line). *Note: Commonly used fractions such as those that might be indicated on ruler, measuring cup, etc.*

NYS Testing Program Modeled Instruction

8 Which group of numbers is ordered from *least* to *greatest*?

F 0.8, 0.52, 0.502, 0.083

G 0.502, 0.52, 0.083, 0.8

H 0.083, 0.502, 0.52, 0.8

J 0.502, 0.52, 0.8, 0.083

Tip: It is easier to order numbers if they all have the same number of decimal places. Add 0s to the right of the last decimal place to give all the numbers the same number of decimal places. Then compare the numbers by writing them in a column with the decimal points lined up.

9 What fraction of the circles are shaded?

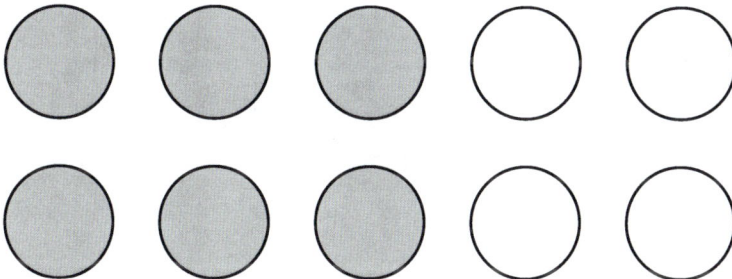

A $\frac{1}{5}$

B $\frac{2}{5}$

C $\frac{3}{5}$

D $\frac{4}{5}$

Tip: A fraction can describe a part of a group. The shaded circles are part of the group of circles. Use the number of shaded circles as the numerator. Remember to write a fraction in simplest form.

New York State Standards
8. **Number Sense and Operations (Content 5.N.8, Process 5.PS.10)**
 Read, write, and order decimals to thousandths
9. **Number Sense and Operations (Content 4.N.8, Process 5.PS.6)**
 Recognize and generate equivalent fractions (halves, fourths, thirds, fifths, sixths, and tenths) using manipulatives, visual models, and illustrations (Post-March)

Go On

10 The chart below models 0.40 + 0.23.

0.01	0.11	0.21	0.31	0.41	0.51	0.61	0.71	0.81	0.91
0.02	0.12	0.22	0.32	0.42	0.52	0.62	0.72	0.82	0.92
0.03	0.13	0.23	0.33	0.43	0.53	0.63	0.73	0.83	0.93
0.04	0.14	0.24	0.34	0.44	0.54	0.64	0.74	0.84	0.94
0.05	0.15	0.25	0.35	0.45	0.55	0.65	0.75	0.85	0.95
0.06	0.16	0.26	0.36	0.46	0.56	0.66	0.76	0.86	0.96
0.07	0.17	0.27	0.37	0.47	0.57	0.67	0.77	0.87	0.97
0.08	0.18	0.28	0.38	0.48	0.58	0.68	0.78	0.88	0.98
0.09	0.19	0.29	0.39	0.49	0.59	0.69	0.79	0.89	0.99
0.10	0.20	0.30	0.40	0.50	0.60	0.70	0.80	0.90	1.00

What is the sum of 0.40 + 0.23?

F 0.17

G 0.50

H 0.60

J 0.63

Tip: The light shaded boxes in the chart represent the first number in the problem, and the dark shaded boxes represent the second number. The shaded box with the greatest number is the sum.

Go On

New York State Standards
10. **Number Sense and Operations (Content 4.N.25, Process 5.PS.3)**
Add and subtract decimals to tenths and hundredths using a hundreds chart (Post-March)

NYS Testing Program Modeled Instruction

11 Carlos has $0.62 in his pocket.

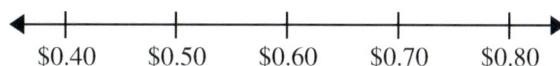

Between which two numbers is $0.62?

A $0.40 and $0.50

B $0.50 and $0.60

C $0.60 and $0.70

D $0.70 and $0.80

Tip: Compare 0.62 to the numbers on the number line. To compare decimals, compare the tenths place. If the tenths place is the same, compare the hundredths place.

12 Below is a chart of 4 different parks and how many acres each park covers.

Park	Number of Acres
Denali	6,075,030
Gates of the Arctic	8,472,506
Glacier Bay	3,283,246
Katmai	4,726,673

Which list names the parks in order from *largest* to *smallest*?

F   Denali, Gates of the Arctic, Glacier Bay, Katmai

G   Gates of the Arctic, Denali, Katmai, Glacier Bay

H   Katmai, Gates of the Arctic, Denali, Glacier Bay

J   Glacier Bay, Katmai, Denali, Gates of the Arctic

Tip: To order numbers, compare the digits in each place value position. Start with the digits in the millions place.

New York State Standards
11. Number Sense and Operations (Content 4.N.12, Process 5.CN.3)
    Use concrete materials and visual models to compare and order decimals (less than 1) to the hundredths place in the context of money (Post-March)
12. Number Sense and Operations (Content 5.N.2, Process 5.CN.9)
    Compare and order numbers to millions

Go On

13 Ryan jogged $\frac{5}{8}$ mile on Monday. On Wednesday, he jogged $\frac{7}{8}$ mile. He jogged $\frac{3}{8}$ mile on Friday. About how many miles did Ryan jog in all?

- **A** $1\frac{1}{2}$ miles
- **B** 2 miles
- **C** $2\frac{1}{2}$ miles
- **D** 3 miles

Tip: First, round each distance to the nearest half mile. Then add the rounded numbers to find about how many miles Ryan jogged in all.

14 Which of the following numbers is prime?

- **F** 6
- **G** 15
- **H** 23
- **J** 62

Tip: A prime number has exactly two factors: 1 and the number itself. A number that has 3 or more factors is composite.

15 What is the value of the expression below?

$$4 + 5 \times 8 - 6 \div 2$$

- **A** 9
- **B** 33
- **C** 41
- **D** 69

Tip: Use the order of operations to evaluate the expression. First, multiply and divide from left to right. Then add and subtract from left to right.

Go On

New York State Standards
13. **Number Sense and Operations (Content 5.N.25, Process 5.CN.6)** Estimate sums and differences of fractions with like denominators
14. **Number Sense and Operations (Content 5.N.12, Process 5.CM.9)** Recognize that some numbers are only divisible by one and themselves (prime) and others have multiple divisors (composite)
15. **Number Sense and Operations (Content 5.N.18, Process 5.PS.3)** Evaluate an arithmetic expression using order of operations including multiplication, division, addition, subtraction, and parentheses

16 The shaded part of which model represents the greatest fraction?

F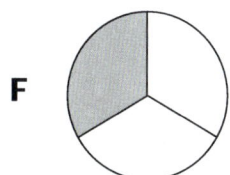

G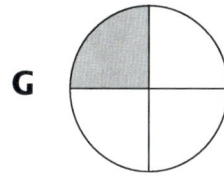

H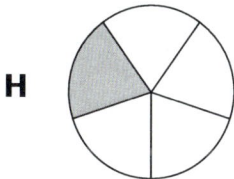

J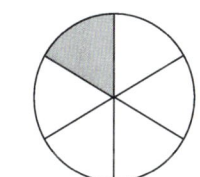

🌀 **Tip:** Each model is divided into a different number of parts. Each model has 1 part shaded. So, 1 is the numerator for each of the fractions. The number of parts each model is divided into is the denominator of the fraction. Write a fraction to represent the shaded part of each model. Compare the fractions to see which is greatest.

17 Which list shows all the factors of 24?

A 1, 24

B 1, 2, 4, 6, 12, 24

C 1, 2, 3, 4, 6, 8, 12, 24

D 1, 2, 3, 4, 6, 8, 10, 12, 14, 24

🌀 **Tip:** When two whole numbers can be multiplied to get a given number, they are factors of the given number. To find all the factors of a number, list all the numbers that divide evenly into the number.

New York State Standards
16. **Number Sense and Operations (Content 4.N.9, Process 5.CN.4)**
Use concrete materials and visual models to compare and order unit fractions or fractions with the same denominator (with and without the use of a number line) (Post-March)
17. **Number Sense and Operations (Content 5.N.14, Process 5.RP.1)**
Identify the factors of a given number

Go On

18 What is 98.33 minus 16.04?

- F 104.37
- G 82.39
- H 82.29
- J 81.29

> **Tip:** Write the problem as numbers in columns. Place the greater number over the lesser number. Align the decimal points. Subtract the digits in each place, from right to left. Regroup as necessary.

19 A 4-digit whole number has a different odd digit in each place. The number 3 appears in the hundreds place. What is the greatest value this number can have?

- A 7,395
- B 7,953
- C 9,375
- D 9,753

> **Tip:** Odd digits are 1, 3, 5, 7, and 9. Draw a place value chart. Write a 3 in the hundreds place. Remember that the thousands place is the greatest place value in a four-digit number. So, the greatest odd digit must be in the thousands place.

20 Which fraction is equivalent to $3\frac{3}{4}$?

- F $\frac{3}{2}$
- G $\frac{9}{4}$
- H $\frac{15}{4}$
- J $\frac{33}{4}$

> **Tip:** Rewrite the mixed number as an improper fraction. Look at the denominator in the fraction of the mixed number. Rewrite the whole number as a fraction using this denominator. Then, add this fraction to the fraction in the mixed number.

Go On

New York State Standards
18. **Number Sense and Operations (Content 5.N.23, Process 5.PS.3)**
    Use a variety of strategies to add, subtract, multiply, and divide decimals to thousandths
19. **Number Sense and Operations (Content 5.N.3, Process 5.PS.3)**
    Understand the place value structure of the base ten number system
    10 ones = 1 ten
    10 tens = 1 hundred
    10 hundreds = 1 thousand
    10 thousands = 1 ten thousand
    10 ten thousands = 1 hundred thousand
    10 hundred thousands = 1 million
20. **Number Sense and Operations (Content 5.N.20, Process 5.R.6)**
    Convert improper fractions to mixed numbers, and mixed numbers to improper fractions

21 Rosa needed a ribbon that was $\frac{2}{3}$ foot long to finish her project for art class. Which fraction is equivalent to $\frac{2}{3}$?

- **A** $\frac{4}{12}$
- **B** $\frac{4}{9}$
- **C** $\frac{11}{8}$
- **D** $\frac{4}{6}$

Tip: An equivalent fraction represents the same part of the whole. To find an equivalent fraction, multiply the numerator and the denominator by the same non-zero number.

22 Kelly, Matt, and Dana have a combined total of 633 baseball cards. If the 3 friends were to divide the baseball cards equally among themselves, how many cards would each friend get?

- **F** 200
- **G** 211
- **H** 231
- **J** 311

Tip: Dividing equally means that each friend would get the same number of cards. Divide the total number of cards by the number of equal groups to be formed.

New York State Standards
21. **Number Sense and Operations (Content 5.N.4, Process 5.R.6)**
    Create equivalent fractions, given a fraction
22. **Number Sense and Operations (Content 5.N.17, Process 5.PS.5)**
    Use a variety of strategies to divide three-digit numbers by one- and two-digit numbers. *Note: Division by anything greater than a two-digit divisor should be done using technology.*

Go On

23

$$\begin{array}{r} 33 \\ \times\ 32 \\ \hline \end{array}$$

- **A** 96
- **B** 192
- **C** 996
- **D** 1,056

> **Tip:** To multiply two 2-digit numbers, first multiply the top number by the value of the one's place in the bottom number. Then multiply the top number by the value of the ten's place in the bottom number. Then add the two products.

24 Tamara wants to estimate the area of a wall in her living room. She measured the wall and wrote the number sentence below.

10.8 feet × 7.2 feet = ☐ square feet

Which is the *best* estimate of the area of the wall?

- **F** 72 square feet
- **G** 77 square feet
- **H** 80 square feet
- **J** 88 square feet

> **Tip:** To estimate the area of the wall, round each measurement to the nearest whole number of feet. Then multiply the rounded measurements.

Go On

New York State Standards
23. Number Sense and Operations (Content 4.N.19, Process 5.CM.11) Use a variety of strategies to multiply two-digit numbers by two-digit numbers (with and without regrouping) (Post-March)
24. Number Sense and Operations (Content 5.N.26, Process 5.CN.6) Estimate sums, differences, products, and quotients of decimals

25 What is the value of the expression $\frac{5}{6} - \frac{1}{6}$?

A $\frac{4}{0}$

B $\frac{2}{6}$

C $\frac{1}{2}$

D $\frac{4}{6}$

> **Tip:** To subtract fractions with the same denominators, subtract the numerators. The difference has the same denominator.

26 Which number can go in the box to make this number sentence true?

$7.620 < \square$

F 7.200

G 7.270

H 7.600

J 7.720

> **Tip:** To compare decimals, compare the place value of the digits from left to right. If the digits in the greatest place value are the same, compare digits in the next place value. Repeat this until you find a place value with digits that are different.

New York State Standards
25. **Number Sense and Operations (Content 4.N.23, Process 5.CM.11)** Add and subtract proper fractions with common denominators (Post-March)
26. **Number Sense and Operations (Content 5.N.10, Process 5.PS.12)** Compare decimals using <, >, or =

Go On

27 A children's museum sold 4,371 tickets in May and 2,784 tickets in June.

Part A

How many total tickets were sold in May and June?

Show your work.

Answer _____ tickets

Part B

Use estimation to check that your answer is reasonable.

Show your work.

Tip: To find the total number of tickets sold, add the number of tickets sold each month. To estimate the number of tickets sold, first round each number of tickets and then add the rounded numbers.

Go On

28 A Web site tracked the number of visitors it had during a three-month period. The results are shown in the chart below.

WEB SITE VISITORS

Month	Visitors
January	12,225
February	9,890
March	15,345

Part A

What was the total number of visitors to the Web site in the three months?

Show your work.

Answer _____ visitors

Part B

Use estimation to justify your answer.

Show your work.

Tip: To find the total number of visitors, add the number of visitors for each month. To estimate the total number of visitors, round each number and then add. Remember, an estimate is reasonable if it is close to the exact amount.

STOP

New York State Standards
28. Number Sense and Operations (Content 5.N.27, Process 5.PS.3)
   Justify the reasonableness of answers using estimation

Lesson 2

Modeled Instruction
Algebra

1 Look at the number line below.

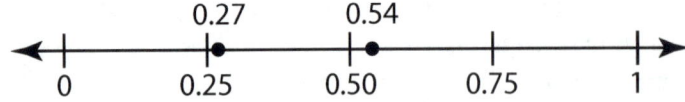

Which statement is true?

A $0.27 < 0.25$

B $0.27 > 0.50$

C $0.54 < 0.75$

D $0.54 < 0.25$

> **Tip:** The symbol > means "greater than," and the symbol < means "less than." On a number line, points are arranged from least to greatest value from left to right.

2 Which number can be placed in the ☐ to make the number sentence true?

$$27 - \square < 20$$

F 3

G 5

H 7

J 8

> **Tip:** The symbol < means "less than." So, the difference of 27 − ☐ must be less than 20.

Go On

New York State Standards
1. **Algebra (Content 4.A.2, Process 5.CM.11)** Use the symbols <, >, =, and ≠ (with and without the use of a number line) to compare whole numbers, unit fractions, and decimals (up to hundredths) (Post-March)
2. **Algebra (Content 4.A.2, Process 5.PS.12)** Use the symbols <, >, =, and ≠ (with and without the use of a number line) to compare whole numbers, unit fractions, and decimals (up to hundredths) (Post-March)

18 ■ NYS Testing Program Modeled Instruction

3 Look at the expression below.

$$4s + 35$$

Part A

What is the variable in the expression?

Answer _____

Part B

What is the constant in the expression?

Answer _____

🌀 **Tip:** A variable is a letter that represents an unknown value. A constant is a value that does not change.

Go On

New York State Standards
3. **Algebra (Content 5.A.1, Process 5.CM.10)** Define and use appropriate terminology when referring to constants, variables, and algebraic expressions

4 Look at this pattern.

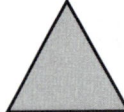

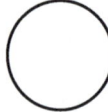

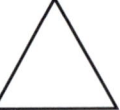

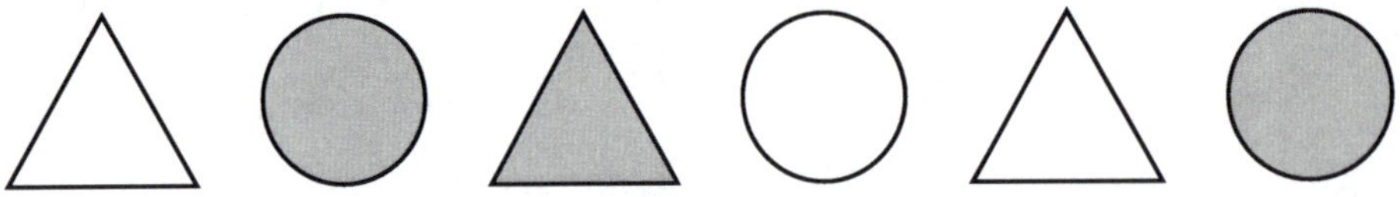

Draw the next 2 figures in the pattern.

Tip: To continue a pattern of shapes, first find the group of shapes that is repeated. Note how many shapes are in the repeating group and what order they appear in. This information gives the "rule" for the pattern.

STOP

New York State Standards

4. **Algebra (Content 5.A.8, Process 5.PS.14)** Create algebraic or geometric patterns using concrete objects or visual drawings (e.g., rotate and shade geometric shapes)

Lesson 3

Modeled Instruction
Geometry

1 Which two triangles appear to be similar?

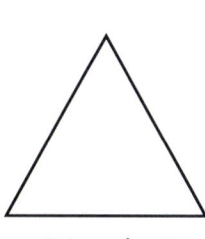 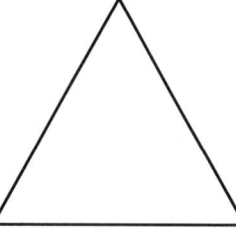  

Triangle Q   Triangle R   Triangle S   Triangle T

- **A** Triangle Q and Triangle R
- **B** Triangle Q and Triangle S
- **C** Triangle R and Triangle S
- **D** Triangle R and Triangle T

> **Tip:** Similar figures have the same shape but may be different sizes. Look for the two triangles that have the same shape and the same angle measurements.

2 What is the perimeter of the figure below?

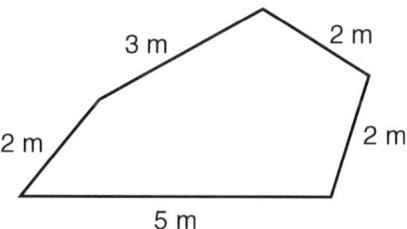

- **F** 8 m
- **G** 9 m
- **H** 13 m
- **J** 14 m

> **Tip:** Perimeter is the distance around a shape or a figure. Use addition to find the perimeter.

Go On

New York State Standards
1. **Geometry (Content 5.G.2, Process 5.CM.10)** Identify pairs of similar triangles
2. **Geometry (Content 5.G.1, Process 5.PS.6)** Calculate the perimeter of regular and irregular polygons

NYS Testing Program Modeled Instruction ■ 21

3 Triangle *FGH* is congruent to triangle *JKL*.

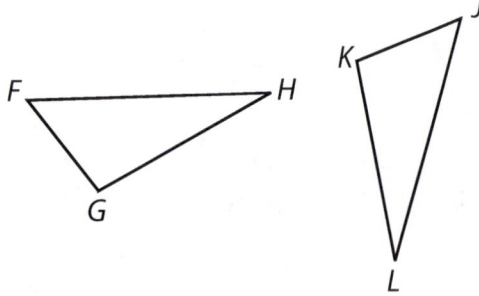

Which side of triangle *JKL* corresponds to side *FG*?

A side *JK*

B side *KL*

C side *LK*

D side *JL*

> **Tip:** Congruent triangles have the same shape and size. Corresponding sides of congruent triangles have the same length.

4 Which shape below has *no* acute angles?

F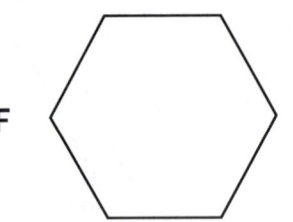

G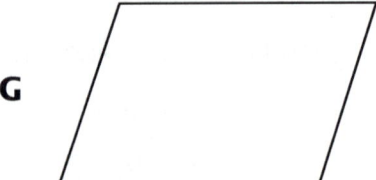

H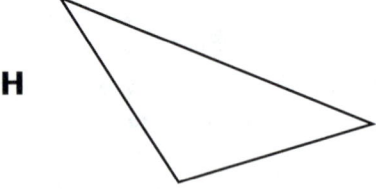

J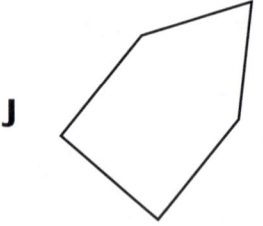

> **Tip:** An acute angle measures less than 90°. Look for the shape without any acute angles.

Go On

New York State Standards
3. **Geometry (Content 5.G.10, Process 5.CM.10)** Identify corresponding parts of congruent triangles
4. **Geometry (Content 4.G.8, Process 5.PS.13)** Classify angles as acute, obtuse, right, and straight (Post-March)

5 Triangle XYZ is similar to triangle QRS.

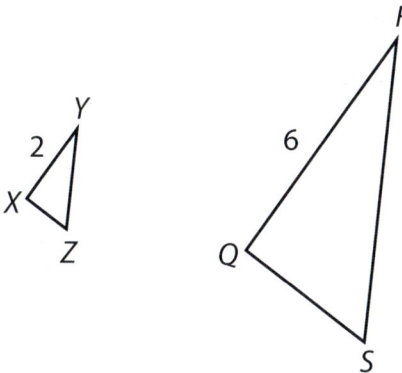

What is the ratio of XY to QR?

A 1:3

B 1:2

C 2:3

D 3:1

Tip: Similar triangles have the same shape and angle measures but do not have to be the same size. The ratio is a comparison of corresponding sides.

6 Which figure has exactly 3 lines of symmetry?

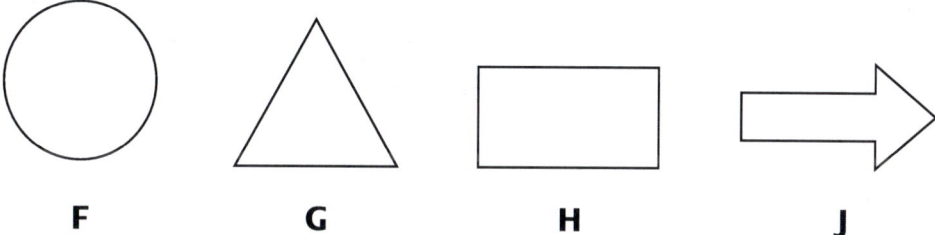

F   G   H   J

Tip: A line of symmetry is an invisible line on which the figure can be folded so that the 2 parts are exactly the same. All the figures have at least 1 line of symmetry. Find the figure with exactly 3.

Go On

New York State Standards
5. Geometry (Content 5.G.3, Process 5.PS.8) Identify the ratio of corresponding sides of similar triangles
6. Geometry (Content 5.G.11, Process 5.PS.13) Identify and draw lines of symmetry of basic geometric shapes

7 Which two triangles are congruent?

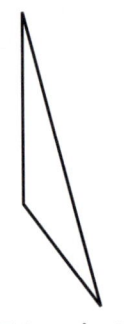 
Triangle 1   Triangle 2

Triangle 3   Triangle 4

A Triangle 1 and Triangle 2
B Triangle 1 and Triangle 3
C Triangle 2 and Triangle 3
D Triangle 2 and Triangle 4

🌀 **Tip:** Congruent figures have the same shape and size. Congruent figures do not have to face the same direction.

8 Which figure below is a rectangle?

F

G

H

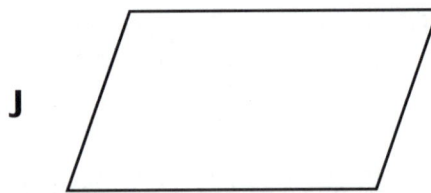
J

🌀 **Tip:** In a rectangle, opposite sides are parallel. Also, in a rectangle, all 4 angles are right angles.

Go On

New York State Standards
7. **Geometry (Content 5.G.9, Process 5.CM.10)** Identify pairs of congruent triangles
8. **Geometry (Content 5.G.4, Process 5.CM.10)** Classify quadrilaterals by properties of their angles and sides

24 ■ NYS Testing Program Modeled Instruction

9 Ally measured the walls in her house and drew the diagram below.

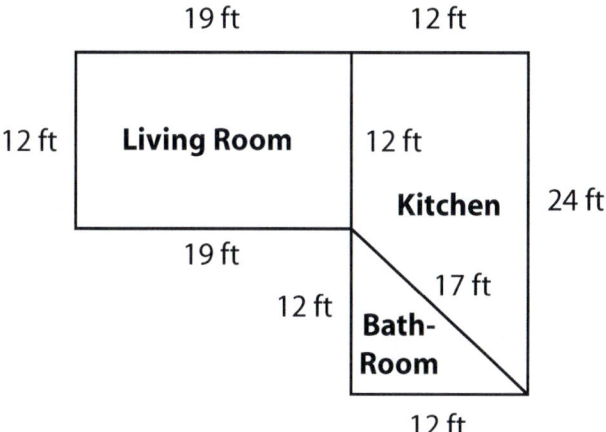

Part A

What is the perimeter of Ally's living room?

Show your work.

Answer _____ ft

Part B

What is the perimeter of Ally's kitchen?

Show your work.

Answer _____ ft

Part C

What is the perimeter of Ally's bathroom?

Show your work.

Answer _____ ft

🌀 **Tip:** Perimeter is the distance around a shape or a figure. To find the perimeter of a room, add the lengths of all the walls of that room.

Go On

New York State Standards
9. **Geometry (Content 5.G.1, Process 5.PS.13)** Calculate the perimeter of regular and irregular polygons

10 What is the missing angle measure in the triangle below?

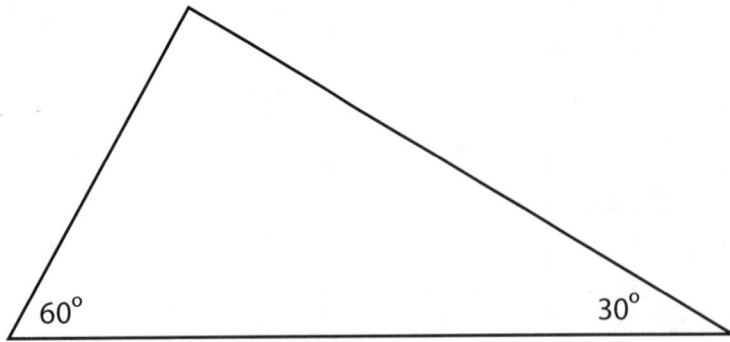

Show your work.

Answer _____

🌀 **Tip:** The sum of the 3 angles in any triangle is 180°. Use subtraction to find the missing angle measure.

11  Use your ruler to help solve this problem.

Part A

Frank drew a pair of parallel lines, and Cathy drew a pair of intersecting lines.

Draw and label what they might have drawn.

Part B

Explain the difference between parallel lines and intersecting lines.

_____

_____

_____

Tip: A line forms a straight path that continues in opposite directions forever. Use the lines drawn in Part A to explain the difference between parallel lines and intersecting lines.

STOP

New York State Standards
11. Geometry (Content 4.G.6, Process 5.CM.3) Draw and identify intersecting, perpendicular, and parallel lines (Post-March)

Lesson 4

Modeled Instruction
Measurement

1 What is the measure of the angle below, to the nearest 5°?

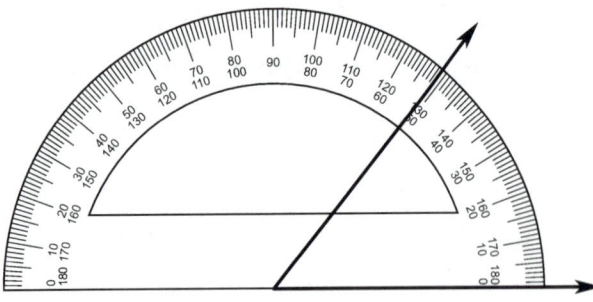

- **A** 50°
- **B** 55°
- **C** 125°
- **D** 130°

> **Tip:** This angle measures less than 90°. To measure an angle that is less than 90°, use the inner scale of the protractor.

2  Use your ruler to help solve this problem.

What is the length of the leaf in centimeters?

- **F** 4 cm
- **G** 5 cm
- **H** 7 cm
- **J** 10 cm

> **Tip:** Line up the left end of the leaf with the 0-cm mark on the ruler. Then read the mark on the ruler at the right end of the leaf.

Go On

New York State Standards
1. **Measurement (Content 5.M.8, Process 5.R.3)** Measure and draw angles using a protractor
2. **Measurement (Content 5.M.3, Process 5.R.4)** Measure to the nearest centimeter

28 ■ NYS Testing Program Modeled Instruction

3 Which of the following is a reasonable estimate for the height of a child?

  A 100 mm

  B 100 cm

  C 100 m

  D 100 km

> **Tip:** Remember how long each unit of measurement is. A millimeter is about the width of a pencil tip. A centimeter is about the length of your thumbnail. A meter is about the same length as three feet. A kilometer is about the same length as half a mile.

4 Which tool below could be used to measure an angle?

F

G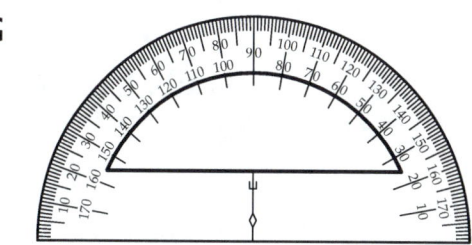

H

J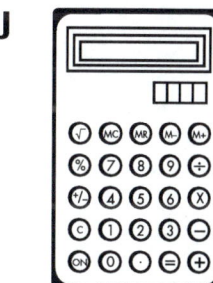

> **Tip:** Different tools are used to find different measurements. Think about what each tool can be used to measure.

New York State Standards
3. **Measurement (Content 5.M.10, Process 5.R.7)** Determine personal references for metric units of length
4. **Measurement (Content 5.M.6, Process 5.PS.13)** Determine the tool and technique to measure with an appropriate level of precision: lengths and angles

5 Mandy estimates that the length of 1 of her steps is about 2 feet. It takes her 52 steps to cross the playground. About how long is the playground in feet?

   A   52 feet

   B   54 feet

   C   104 feet

   D   208 feet

> **Tip:** Since the question asks *about* how long the playground is, you need to find an estimate. Use multiplication to find *about* how long the playground is.

6 Use your ruler to help solve this problem.

How long is the piece of chalk below, measured to the nearest $\frac{1}{4}$ inch?

Answer _____ inches

> **Tip:** Line up one end of the chalk with the 0-inch mark on your ruler. Then read the $\frac{1}{4}$-inch mark that is closest to the other end of the chalk.

New York State Standards
5. **Measurement (Content 5.M.9, Process 5.R.7)** Determine personal references for customary units of length (e.g., your pace is approximately 3 feet, your height is approximately 5 feet, etc.)
6. **Measurement (Content 5.M.1, Process 5.R.4)** Use a ruler to measure to the nearest inch, $\frac{1}{2}$, $\frac{1}{4}$, and $\frac{1}{8}$ inch

Go On

30 ■ NYS Testing Program Modeled Instruction

7 Kendrick went to the store at 2:00. He left the store at the time shown below.

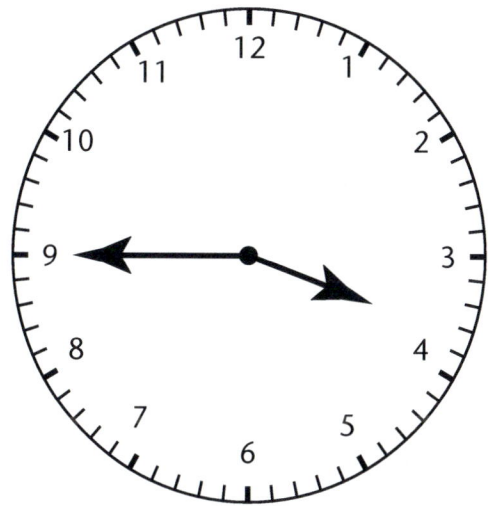

How long did Kendrick spend at the store?

Show your work.

Answer _____

🌀 **Tip:** Read the time shown on the clock. Then count the number of hours and minutes from 2:00 to that time. Skip count by 5s to read minutes.

New York State Standards
7. **Measurement (Content 5.M.7, Process 5.R.1)** Calculate elapsed time in hours and minutes

Go On

8 Use your ruler to help solve this problem.

Look at the rectangle below. The length of the shaded part is 2 cm.

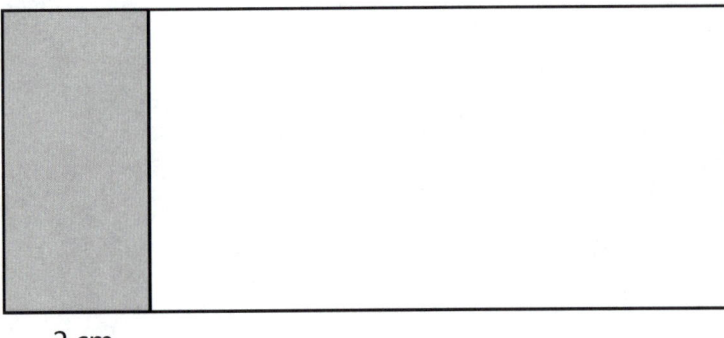

2 cm

Part A

Using the shaded section, estimate the length and width of the rectangle.

Answer _____

Part B

Use your ruler to measure the actual length and width of the rectangle.

Answer _____

Explain why your estimate is reasonable.

_____

_____

_____

> **Tip:** To estimate the length of the rectangle, estimate how many shaded squares would fit in the rectangle. Estimate how many times greater the length of the rectangle is than the length of the shaded square. Then, use your ruler to measure the actual length and width.

STOP

New York State Standards
8. Measurement (Content 5.M.11, Process 5.R.4) Justify the reasonableness of estimates

Lesson 5

Modeled Instruction
Statistics and Probability

1 Mike recorded the daily high temperature every day for 4 days. The temperatures were 75°, 101°, 93°, and 87°. What was the mean of the daily high temperatures for those 4 days?

- **A** 93°
- **B** 89°
- **C** 87°
- **D** 79°

> **Tip:** The mean of a set of data is the sum of the data divided by the number of data items.

2 Sergio wants to know which of these lunches is the most popular at his school: pizza, chicken strips, or grilled cheese sandwich. Which of these is the best way to find out?

- **F** ask friends in his class
- **G** ask students from each grade
- **H** ask friends on his soccer team
- **J** ask students at his lunch table

> **Tip:** Sergio wants to find the most popular lunch at his entire school. So, he must survey the group of students that best represents the entire school.

3 The line graph shows the high temperatures for 8 days in May.

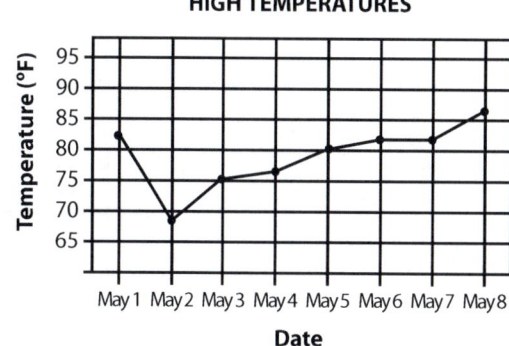

What was the increase in high temperature from May 3rd to May 5th?

- **A** 1° F
- **B** 5° F
- **C** 10° F
- **D** 15° F

> **Tip:** Find May 3rd and May 5th along the bottom of the graph. Then find the high temperatures for each date along the left side of the graph. Use subtraction to find the difference between the high temperatures.

New York State Standards
1. Statistics and Probability (Content 5.S.3, Process 5.R.7) Calculate the mean for a given set of data and use to describe a set of data
2. Statistics and Probability (Content 4.S.1, Process 5.CM.2) Design investigations to address a question from given data (Post-March)
3. Statistics and Probability (Content 5.S.2, Process 5.PS.14) Display data in a line graph to show an increase or a decrease over time

Go On

4 Samantha plays in a basketball league. The table below shows her scores in her first 6 games.

SAMANTHA'S POINTS

Game	Number of Points
1	10
2	12
3	8
4	15
5	16
6	17

Part A

What is the mean number of points Samantha scored per game?

Show your work.

Answer _____ points

Part B

Trish plays in the same league as Samantha. Trish scored a mean of 10 points per game in the first 6 games. Which girl scored the most points during the first 6 games?

Answer _____

Explain your answer.

_____

_____

_____

💡 **Tip:** To find the mean of a given set of data, first add all the numbers in the data set. Then divide this sum by the amount of numbers in the data set.

STOP

New York State Standards
4. Statistics and Probability (Content 5.S.3, Process 5.CN.9)
   Calculate the mean for a given set of data and use to describe a set of data

Grade 5

New York State Testing Program

Mathematics Practice Test Session 1

TIPS FOR TAKING THE TEST

Follow these suggestions to do well on the test:

- Be sure to read all the directions carefully.
- Ask your teacher for help with any directions you do not understand.
- Use your tools whenever they will help you solve a problem on the test.
- Read each question carefully and think about your answer before you write it.

This symbol means to use your ruler.

Session 1

Sample A

$$\begin{array}{r} 347 \\ \times\ 120 \\ \hline \end{array}$$

- **A** 1,041
- **B** 4,164
- **C** 30,640
- **D** 41,640

Sample B

Look at the polygon below.

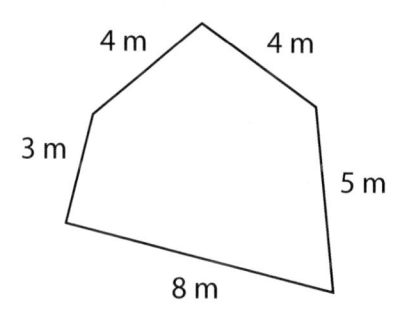

What is the perimeter?

- **F** 4 m
- **G** 16 m
- **H** 24 m
- **J** 34 m

Sample C

Trisha started work at 1:00. She worked for 5 hours 30 minutes. Which clock shows the time Trisha finished work?

A

B

C

D

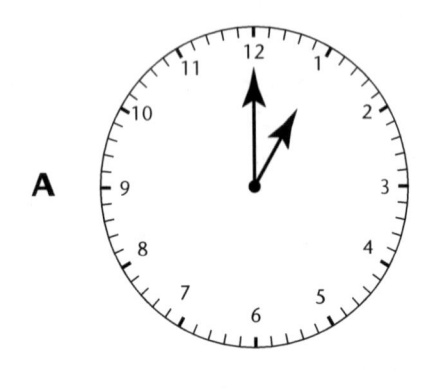

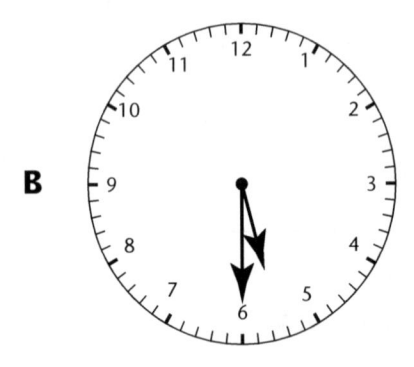

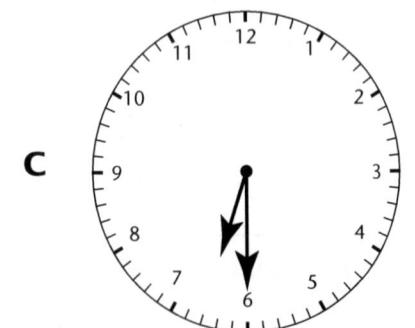

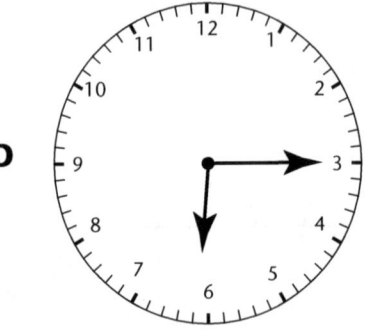

STOP

1 Mt. Marcy is 5,344 feet tall. What is the height of Mt. Marcy in feet, rounded to the nearest hundred?

   A 5,000 feet

   B 5,300 feet

   C 5,400 feet

   D 5,500 feet

2
$$\begin{array}{r} 12 \\ \times\ 20 \\ \hline \end{array}$$

   F 20

   G 32

   H 240

   J 260

3 A rectangular swimming pool is 32 feet long and 16 feet wide. Using the formula $P = 2l + 2w$, where l is the length and w is the width, what is the perimeter P of the swimming pool?

   A 48 feet

   B 96 feet

   C 256 feet

   D 512 feet

Go On

Session 1 — NYS Testing Program Practice Test

4 Carole asked the students in her class how many pets they had. She started to record the results of the survey in the tally table below.

PET SURVEY

Number of Pets	Number of Students
0	卌 |||
1	卌 卌	
2	卌 卌
3	卌
4 or more	

If 6 students had 4 or more pets, what should Carole record in the column "Number of Students?"

F ||||

G 卌

H 卌 |

J 卌 ||

5 What is eight million, seventy-four thousand, thirty-two written in standard form?

A 8,074,032

B 8,074,320

C 8,740,032

D 8,740,320

Go On

6 A football field is 100 yards long. How many feet long is a football field?

- **F** 33 feet
- **G** 100 feet
- **H** 300 feet
- **J** 1000 feet

7 Darius drew a triangle in which two of the angles each measured 80°. What was the measure of the third angle?

- **A** 20°
- **B** 40°
- **C** 60°
- **D** 80°

8 What kind of triangle always has at least two sides of equal length?

- **F** acute
- **G** right
- **H** scalene
- **J** isosceles

9 Which number sentence is true?

A $\frac{3}{4} < \frac{5}{8}$

B $\frac{5}{16} < \frac{3}{8}$

C $\frac{1}{3} = \frac{3}{12}$

D $\frac{1}{5} = \frac{4}{15}$

10 What is the measure of ∠Y in the quadrilateral below?

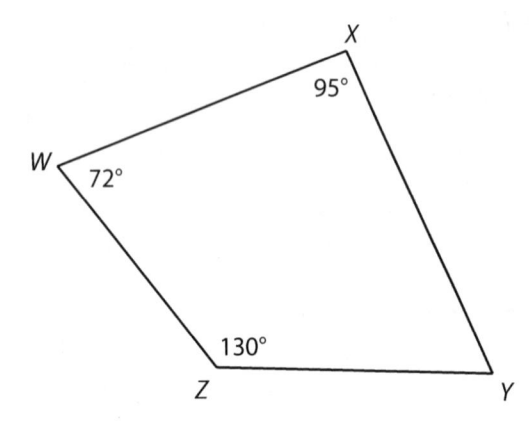

F   3°

G   50°

H   63°

J   95°

11 Sebastian correctly answered 75% of the problems on his math test. Which shows his test score written as a fraction?

A $\frac{1}{4}$

B $\frac{5}{7}$

C $\frac{3}{4}$

D $\frac{7}{5}$

Go On

12 Chen checked his heart rate over several hours. He made a line graph to show the number of heartbeats per minute at each hour.

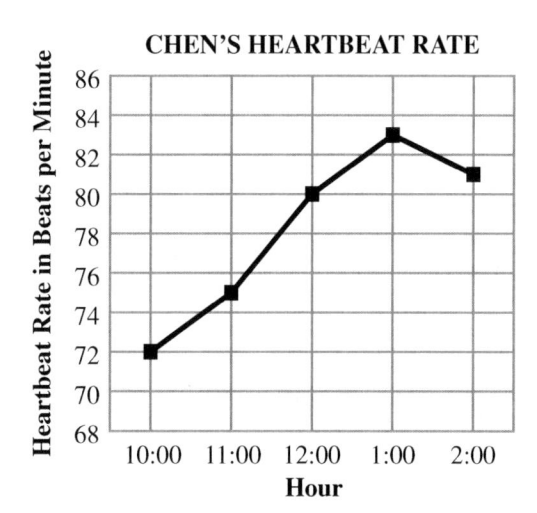

CHEN'S HEARTBEAT RATE

Between which hours did Chen's heartbeat rate decrease?

F 10:00 and 11:00

G 11:00 and 12:00

H 12:00 and 1:00

J 1:00 and 2:00

13 Which number is a multiple of 4?

A 14

B 26

C 27

D 36

Go On

Session 1 NYS Testing Program Practice Test ■ 43

14 Which of the following angles is obtuse?

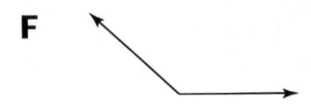

F

G

H

J

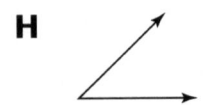

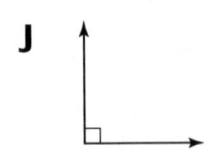

15 Lewis drew a triangle and measured the interior angles. What is the sum of the angles that Lewis measured?

A   90°

B   180°

C   270°

D   360°

Go On

16 What decimal represents the fraction of squares that are shaded?

- F 0.04
- G 0.06
- H 0.4
- J 0.6

17 $\frac{2}{7} + \frac{3}{7}$

- A $\frac{2}{7}$
- B $\frac{3}{7}$
- C $\frac{5}{7}$
- D $\frac{6}{7}$

18 Kenya is making lemonade. To make the lemonade, she needs 1 quart of water. She only has a 1-cup measuring glass. How many cups of water will Kenya need to use?

- F 2 cups
- G 3 cups
- H 4 cups
- J 5 cups

Go On

Session 1 NYS Testing Program Practice Test

19 Which of the following fractions is equivalent to 0.80?

A $\frac{1}{5}$

B $\frac{1}{4}$

C $\frac{4}{5}$

D $\frac{9}{10}$

20 Jenny's family left home at 9:15 A.M. When they got to her grandmother's house, the time was 11:02 A.M. How long did the trip take?

F 2 hours 13 minutes

G 1 hour 47 minutes

H 1 hour 33 minutes

J 17 minutes

21 Which fraction could Point A represent on the number line?

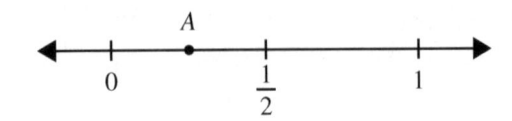

A $\frac{1}{8}$

B $\frac{1}{4}$

C $\frac{1}{2}$

D $\frac{3}{4}$

22 Which best describes an angle?

    F a straight figure with two endpoints

    G a straight figure that continues forever in both directions

    H two rays with the same endpoint

    J two lines that never cross and stay the same distance apart

23 Which is equivalent to the ratio 2 to 3?

    A 1:3

    B 2:3

    C 2:5

    D 3:2

24 A pine tree is 2.6 meters tall. What is the tree's height in centimeters?

    F 0.26

    G 26

    H 260

    J 2,600

Go On

25 Use your ruler to help solve this problem.

What is the measure of the line segment below to the nearest quarter inch?

_____

A 2 inches

B $2\frac{1}{4}$ inches

C $2\frac{3}{4}$ inches

D 3 inches

26 What is the greatest common factor of 40 and 56?

F 2

G 4

H 8

J 20

STOP

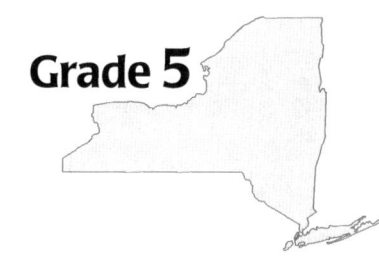

Grade 5 New York State Testing Program

Mathematics Practice Test Session 2

TIPS FOR TAKING THE TEST

Follow these suggestions to do well on the test:
- Be sure to read all the directions carefully.
- Ask your teacher for help with any directions you do not understand.
- Use your tools whenever they will help you solve a problem on the test.
- Read each question carefully and think about your answer before you write it.

This symbol means to use your ruler.

Session 2

27 Betty recorded the morning temperature for 12 days. The list below shows the temperatures.

53°, 58°, 60°, 56°, 61°, 65°
68°, 70°, 72°, 69°, 67°, 64°

Betty began to organize the data in a table.

Part A

Complete the table.

Temperature	Number of Days
From 50° to 59°	3
From 60° to 69°	_____
From 70° to 79°	_____

Part B

Explain how you found your answer.

_____

_____

_____

_____

Go On

28 Carlos mows the lawn to earn his allowance. His parents give him one 5-dollar bill, one 1-dollar bill, and two quarters each month for mowing.

Part A

Write the amount Carlos earns in number form.

Part B

Write the amount Carlos earns in word form.

Go On

29 These are the first 4 figures in a pattern.

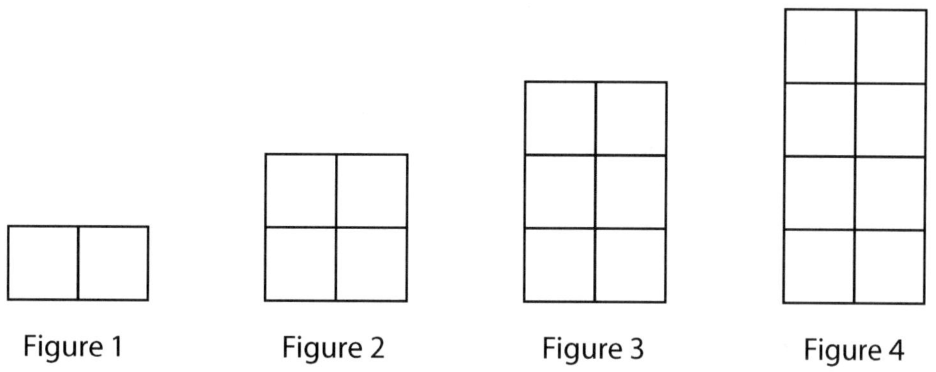

Figure 1   Figure 2   Figure 3   Figure 4

Part A

Write a rule that can be used to find the number of blocks for any figure in the pattern.

Part B

How many blocks will the seventh figure have?

30 Look at the following pattern of dots.

●
○ ○
● ● ●
○ ○ ○ ○
● ○　● ○ ●　● ○ ● ○ ●　● ○ ● ○ ●
Figure 1　Figure 2　Figure 3　　Figure 4

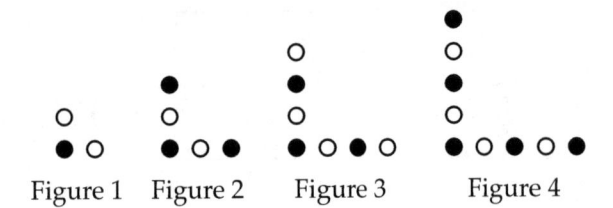

Draw the next 2 figures in the pattern.

Go On

54 ■ NYS Testing Program Practice Test　Session 2

31 Daniel drew two lines that intersected to form right angles.

Part A

How can Daniel best describe the two lines he drew?

_____

_____

_____

Part B

Draw two lines the way Daniel might have drawn them.

Go On

32 The graph below shows the population of Nortown over a 50-year period.

POPULATION IN NORTOWN OVER 50 YEARS

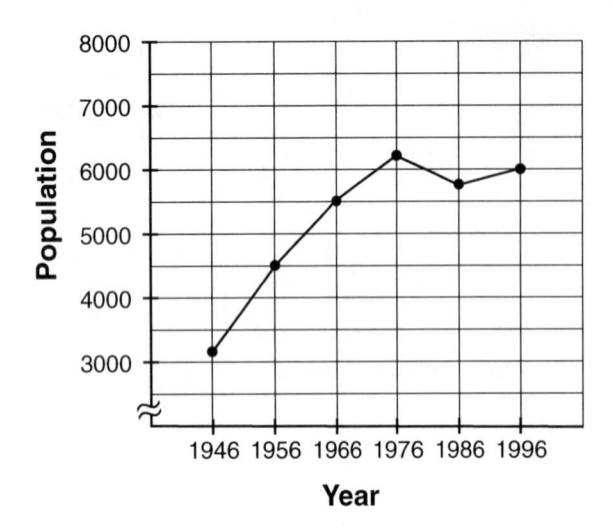

Part A

In what year was the population of Nortown double what it was in 1946?

Part B

What would you estimate the population of Nortown to be in the year 2006?

33 As student body president, Eddie is setting up a table in the cafeteria for students to sign up for the school clean-up drive. His table has the shape shown below.

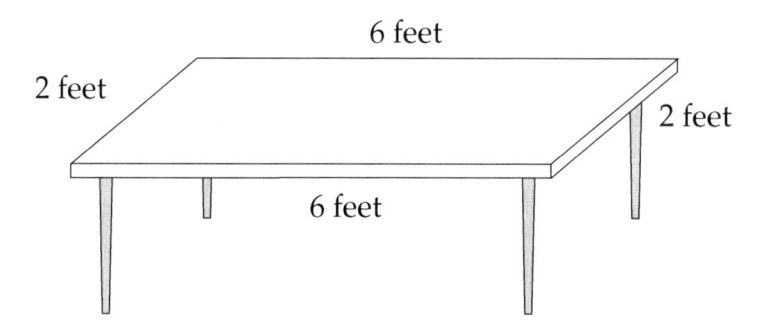

(Diagram of a rectangular table: 6 feet long, 2 feet wide)

Part A

Eddie wants to put a string of lights around the edge of his table. How many feet of lights will he need?

Show your work.

Part B

Eddie has a second table that is 2 feet longer and 2 feet wider than the table shown in Part A. How many feet of lights will he need to go around the edge of the second table?

Show your work.

34 All regular polygons have lines of symmetry. There is a relationship between the number of sides a regular polygon has and the number of lines of symmetry it has.

Part A

How many lines of symmetry does this triangle have? Draw them.

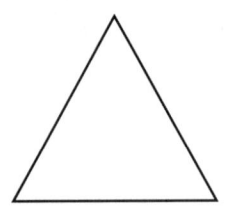

Part B

How many lines of symmetry does this square have? Draw them.

Part C

How many lines of symmetry would a regular 10-sided polygon have?

Cut-Out Tools

NYS Testing Program Practice Test ■ 59

NYS Testing Program Answer Sheet

STUDENT'S NAME		SCHOOL:
LAST	FIRST MI	TEACHER:
		FEMALE ○ MALE ○

BIRTH DATE

MONTH	DAY	YEAR
Jan ○	⓪ ⓪	⓪ ⓪
Feb ○	① ①	① ①
Mar ○	② ②	② ②
Apr ○	③ ③	③ ③
May ○	④	④ ④
Jun ○	⑤	⑤ ⑤
Jul ○	⑥	⑥ ⑥
Aug ○	⑦	⑦ ⑦
Sep ○	⑧	⑧ ⑧
Oct ○	⑨	⑨ ⑨
Nov ○		
Dec ○		

GRADE ③ ④ ⑤ ⑥ ⑦ ⑧

Achieve
New York State
Mathematics
Grade 5

The New York State assessments in Mathematics are published by CTB/McGraw-Hill. Such company has neither endorsed nor authorized this test-preparation book.

PRACTICE TEST
Session 1

1 Ⓐ Ⓑ Ⓒ Ⓓ   6 Ⓕ Ⓖ Ⓗ Ⓙ   11 Ⓐ Ⓑ Ⓒ Ⓓ   16 Ⓕ Ⓖ Ⓗ Ⓙ   21 Ⓐ Ⓑ Ⓒ Ⓓ   26 Ⓕ Ⓖ Ⓗ Ⓙ
2 Ⓕ Ⓖ Ⓗ Ⓙ   7 Ⓐ Ⓑ Ⓒ Ⓓ   12 Ⓕ Ⓖ Ⓗ Ⓙ   17 Ⓐ Ⓑ Ⓒ Ⓓ   22 Ⓕ Ⓖ Ⓗ Ⓙ
3 Ⓐ Ⓑ Ⓒ Ⓓ   8 Ⓕ Ⓖ Ⓗ Ⓙ   13 Ⓐ Ⓑ Ⓒ Ⓓ   18 Ⓕ Ⓖ Ⓗ Ⓙ   23 Ⓐ Ⓑ Ⓒ Ⓓ
4 Ⓕ Ⓖ Ⓗ Ⓙ   9 Ⓐ Ⓑ Ⓒ Ⓓ   14 Ⓕ Ⓖ Ⓗ Ⓙ   19 Ⓐ Ⓑ Ⓒ Ⓓ   24 Ⓕ Ⓖ Ⓗ Ⓙ
5 Ⓐ Ⓑ Ⓒ Ⓓ   10 Ⓕ Ⓖ Ⓗ Ⓙ   15 Ⓐ Ⓑ Ⓒ Ⓓ   20 Ⓕ Ⓖ Ⓗ Ⓙ   25 Ⓐ Ⓑ Ⓒ Ⓓ

Session 2
Answer open-ended questions directly in the book.